A Hunger For Wholeness

A Hunger For Wholeness

Joan Hutson

AVE MARIA PRESS Notre Dame, Indiana 46556

Library of Congress Catalog Card Number: 77-93017
International Standard Book Number: 0-87793-145-3

Design and typography: Cae Esworthy
Illustrations by the author.

Printed and bound in the United States of America.

Contents

To the Father 7

SELF-LOVE 8

PRIDE 12

ENVY 16

INDIFFERENCE 20

GREED 24

INFERIORITY 28

SUPERIORITY 32

INDEPENDENCE 36

DESPONDENCY 40

TALKATIVENESS 44

SMALLNESS 48

INORDINATE AMBITION 52

DEFENSIVENESS 56

DISHONESTY 60

FAITHLESSNESS 64

EXCESSIVENESS 68

CONFLICTING SELVES 72

PASSIVENESS 76

FEAR OF SUFFERING 80

To the Son 87

To the Father

LORD, I hunger to be one in you. I ask you to help me redirect, with your gentle promptings, all the forces within me that oppose this longing. May the plan of creation you had in mind for me be perfectly rendered. I join with you in saying, "Let there be me."

Self-Love

SELF-LOVE, your voice is never still. I couldn't begin to determine how shattering your incessant suggestions have been, and how blindly I have listened to your imprisoning thoughts. How often I have fallen under the sweep of your subtle, specious arguments. How often you have convinced me that I must satisfy my own needs first, for only then will I be perfectly positioned to hear the cries of others.

This always sounded like plausible reasoning, and I cooperated with your promptings. Now I see that the more I try to satisfy my needs, the more needs there are to satisfy. What I once considered luxury, I now classify as need. You have me so absorbed in feeding my false hunger that I hardly recognize the cry of true hunger.

You have treacherous plans, SELF-LOVE, for the more satisfactions you manage to achieve, the more demanding you become. It is so easy for me to justify you as you insinuate your gentle ideas. When your suggestions have become realities, you tenderly apply the balm of *justification* so I do not have to feel selfish.

Where will you lead, O tormenting force whose enslavement frightens me? I am not the only one who suffers from the blind obedience you exact. Whenever you are threatened by outside forces, you, through me, attempt to annihilate whatever causes you to feel uneasy about your position. How many people I have pushed out of their place in the sun and thrown into shadow because you needed more room to expand, SELF-LOVE. How insatiable your appetite.

I am too exhausted to keep ahead of your cries. I am too worn out to pay your prices any longer. You can dangle your wares before me, but I won't be infatuated with your promises any longer. All you have ever offered me has been within the power of the world to take away from me. I am tired of holding covetously all these temporal wares, never daring to relax my grip for fear of someone wresting my treasures from my greed-stiffened grasp.

What can I do, SELF-LOVE, to employ you on my side? Isn't there some facet of you that I could capitalize on, one that could work for my salvation instead of my extinction? Perhaps, if you made me love myself as God intended, my self-love would have its true focus. I would still see myself, but as a transparent self. I would see through myself to God. The God-image would eclipse the self-image. With the God-image forever bleeding through the self-image, I could give you free rein, SELF-LOVE, for soon your tastes would be purified to crave only what the God-image selects.

O blissful freedom, will you ever be mine? SELF-LOVE, refocus, and let's try.

Pride

PRIDE, I am going to wrest myself free from your demanding grip. You insist that I fortify my precious self-image with steel armor, lest I break myself against some shattering rock of reality. Too many times you have kept me from saying the word that would have comforted, the word that would have enlightened, the word that would have encouraged . . . all because you convinced me I might be hurt as I reached out. As long as I submit to being shackled by your dictates, I will never experience life.

I am breaking the security cage you have laminated around me. I am coming out to face the vicissitudes of life. The bright lights may blind me; the dark nights may bewilder me; the cacophony around me may offend my long-sheltered ears, but I am coming out to meet all of this.

I am coming out defenseless. I know that my God will temper the wind to the shorn lamb. I am going to know what it is to be forsaken, misunderstood, maligned, rejected, and unappreciated.

I am going to grow, and it is you, PRIDE, I am asking to help me to my new expectations. You have the qualifications. You can listen to God's word and with the same desire for perfection that protected me from life, you are going to lead me through his will. With your zeal, we are going to strive for eternal values rather than temporary comfort.

No longer will I fear to think, speak, or act in dread of

splintering the shimmering crystal of prideful living. Now the whole world is my habitat . . . the ugly as well as the beautiful, the profane as well as the refined, the insulted as well as the respected. I embrace them all to help me grow in Christ.

In weariness, my weariness shall serve him; in degradation, my degradation shall serve him, in bewilderment, my bewilderment shall serve him; in joy, my joy shall serve him.

PRIDE, are you ready?

Envy

ENVY, uninvited guest, what unrest you engender in my heart! You blind me to all the gifts God has given me, and ask me to concentrate instead on all the gifts he has not given me, but has given others. I trip over untapped resources at my feet, and gaze longingly at the dazzling gifts of others.

Oh, if I only had the appearance of that brilliantly attractive one; oh, if I only had the astute wisdom of that scholarly one; oh, if I only had the social presence of that confident one. That is how you speak to me, ENVY.

My heart is saying softly, "Let me be me. I was created in God's image. Something about me reflects the Father."

Is it my patience, my understanding, my smile, my voice, my love for others? I have a glorious commission to reflect mementos of the Father to a world which often feels Fatherless. I must strive to discover that special facet of him that he expects me to reflect, and no longer be blinded by the scintillating brilliance of the facets of others.

While I warm myself at the blazing fire of others' talents, my flame grows weaker and dimmer, and sometimes is extinguished. I become a smoldering wick whose angry smoke writhes in envy and scorn. In this torture of the moment, I am lost in my own obscurity.

ENVY, you are powerful. What role could you play that would be virtuous? You could set before me the virtues that lead to holiness. You could make me burn with your unrest

18

and zeal, envious eyes fixed on perfection in faith, hope, and love. Yes, give me no rest, as you have given me no rest in the past, until I have reached the perfection I long for. Fire me with such envy to possess these virtues that no price is too high to pay. As you have so often done in the past, enlist my physical strength to work beyond endurance. But now, instead of exhausting me in the envious pursuit of honor, prestige, brilliance of mind, charm and worldly grace, exhaust me in the pursuit of the virtues that will enable me to reflect my Father to the world, for I am wondrously made in his divine image.

Indifference

INDIFFERENCE, you have, with soft blankets, made me so warm and comfortable. You have even tucked my conscience into your warm embrace so that it doesn't want to respond to any calls which would interrupt the lullaby. I know the world is out there calling, but I keep turning the alarm off so my dreams can continue. Reality out there is going to cost me something. INDIFFERENCE, I want to pull you like a mantle down over my head. I want to remain peaceful.

Sometimes I calculate a case, and if it won't demand too much of me, I reach out a little. This helps to appease my not quite dead-asleep conscience. INDIFFERENCE, you do make life simpler for me. If I responded with enthusiasm to all that life calls me to, I would be weary from serving. You help deaden the cries that reach my consciousness; you still my voice that is sometimes prompted to speak up for righteousness; you suggest that I turn away when I see evil triumph . . . you save me costly involvement.

You are also making sin smaller and smaller. You are widening the way that God called the "narrow way." I am really not walking any path now. I am lying still in the plain wrapper of indifference. I don't care enough to hurt, and I don't hurt enough to care. I don't listen enough to hear, and I don't hear enough to listen.

What Jesus said about the lukewarm frightens me. He said it would be better to be hot or cold, but never lukewarm. INDIFFERENCE, I have a role for you in my life. I see a light of possibility in you. I am calling on you to make me in-different to some aspects of my life. I want to be indifferent toward amassing material possessions, indifferent toward gaining popular support, indifferent toward idle curiosity and passing vanities.

I am calling on you, INDIFFERENCE, to help me gain indifference in these areas. But I want to lose you in the areas that are giving me a false peace, a peace that doesn't see or hear the needs of others around me, a peace that remains silent when it ought to scream for justice, a peace that excuses sin and waters down remorse. INDIFFERENCE, I cannot thank you for false peace, but I do enlist your services in the fight against worldly allurements that make me indifferent toward God's will for me.

Greed

GREED, you are pushing me headlong into many areas that deliberation would hold me back from. You act in a torrential rush, and my hands are clasped around a goal before reason has had time to discern. My hands are filled even before I realize I am reaching. Then I look at my filled hands and am appalled at their emptiness.

Where are the joy and contentment that you promised? GREED, you work so fast that reason is inundated by your destructive floodwaters and cannot stand in your path. Your relentless fury is not stayed by any words of conscience, by any friends, or even by God himself. Your promises are empty.

I don't want the object I hold, you can have that. I want the happiness you promised it would bring. Instead I have the shame and guilt of admitting how much time, effort and anxiety you have caused me. I have the remorse of knowing I have been tricked by you, GREED.

I cannot listen to your dictates any longer. The goods you have insisted I amass are suffocating me. All around are empty crates of what you ordered for my happiness. I am trapped by them, and I scream for the four winds to blow away all the disappointing chaff around me. North wind, take all the material possessions that taunt me with their haunting nothingness. South wind, take away the shallow friendships I founded only to feel supported and protected. East wind, drive away all the attitudes I have stored up to be shielded from the sharp turns of reality. West winds, blow away the density that obscures my vision of God, for when I see him clearly, GREED will also be seen for what it is . . . a charlatan.

GREED, I see one use for you in my life. I ask you to make me greedy for treasures in heaven. Inspire me to pile up treasure where thief cannot rob, nor moth consume. Let me be as quick to recognize opportunity for winning God's favor as I have been quick to grasp opportunities to serve self. Oh GREED, if I can transform your insatiable appetite for worldly treasure into an unquenchable hunger for the things of God, I will someday thank you for all you did for me.

Inferiority

INFERIORITY, you are draining away my hope. You are insidiously cutting away at the only real lifeline that I have: the belief that God loves me. You have succeeded in stripping away any belief in my self-worth. You have shown me—in countless ways!—how worthless I am.

I could easily cave in on the nothingness you have convinced me I am. You have reduced me to clay that even dares ask the Potter, "Why have you used such gross material in forming this vessel of me?" You have focused a distorting light on me: it brings my shortcomings into sharp focus, and fades out any good I might have dwelt on to save my self-image.

This same light is causing me to close my hurting eyes to the one healing Light that could save me. You have almost convinced me that he would refuse to look at his depraved child, the one he isn't proud to call his own.

INFERIORITY, you have shattered my life and I am not sure I care to pick up the pieces of brokenness. If I could manage to piece myself together again, I could never bear the polishing it would take to make myself shine with self-worth.

God has said so many things to help me see value in myself. He said, "I have loved YOU with an everlasting love." "Even if a mother should forget her child, I will not forget YOU." INFERIORITY, I don't see how you can win over these sacred words with your arguments. I cannot understand your

30

power to convince me that he didn't include ME in these promises of love.

Yet, even though I cannot withstand your arguments of my unworthiness, you have put me in the best position to receive his love. He said, "I have come to call the sinner"; "I came that the sinner might live, not die"; "I will search for the one who is lost until I find him."

Somehow, INFERIORITY, you have convinced me that I fit in this category. With the publican I will say, "Lord I am not worthy. I know that I am your child, and any thought that makes me believe that you don't love me I am going to drown in the redemptive blood that flowed for me from your side on Calvary."

INFERIORITY, perhaps you helped to make me humble, but I am going to dismiss you now, with a questionable "thank you," and cling to this hope: "The proud he turns away empty, the humble he fills with himself."

Superiority

SUPERIORITY, there may be more danger in you than in your complement, INFERIORITY. You make me the Pharisee in the parable of self-righteousness. You blind me to what I really am. You excuse all I do or don't do; you give me a poisonous pity for those of lesser stature. You stealthily watch lest someone from the lower ranks dare raise himself to your level. You harshly criticize actions from the lower ranks which suddenly become virtuous if done by you on your more lofty level.

You never leave me in peace, SUPERIORITY, for I always find others around me capable of moving me out of the highest place. I have a constant battle to stay at the top. What a life of bondage this is! Everywhere I go, I must be the epitome of excellence. Others must notice that I am not just ordinary. You have made me feel lost in the crowd unless I am acknowledged as graciously gifted. You make me dwell on some aspect of my greatness, or else make me lose my self-identity. Then I must scramble mentally for some reinforcements of greatness, some reassurances that I am in a class to be envied.

When there is someone around who excels me, how enraged you become, SUPERIORITY. How frantic you become as you try to stabilize your tottering hold. You minimize the greatness I see in others, you try to hold their glory down. The thought of being toppled from your lofty throne suggests and supports all kinds of unjust tyranny. When you see for sure that you cannot hold your position any longer, you steal away so your defeat is imperceptible—even to yourself.

SUPERIORITY, you have damaged my life long enough. The only area I will give you room to work in is this: Make me SUPERIOR in my *need* for God's grace, for indeed you have led me to a haughtiness that needs God's mercy and grace.

He said that he would humble the exalted, and surely you have made me exalted. He also said that he would not spurn a contrite heart . . . and so I go to him for help.

You, SUPERIORITY, are going to work now on my behalf, by towering over all else in the need to be humbled by God's redeeming grace. You will get the attention that you have thrived on all these years, but now you are going to be known as the one who needs God's grace most. You are supreme in this need. You may not like this new throne, but you will remain there until you have led me as deeply into humility as you have led me to superiority. The journey will be long.

Independence

INDEPENDENCE, all my life you have made me wonder why Jesus said, "Where two or three are gathered in my name, there am I." All my life I have wanted to walk alone to God. The words of Jesus — "What you do for others, you do for me; love one another, for by this I judge your love for me; whoever gives a cup of water in my name will be rewarded," — these words get in my way.

I hear your drum-beat, INDEPENDENCE, but I have lost the pulse of human nature around me. I have pulled so far away from the community of people that you ask me to serve, that no one dares ask me for that drink of water in your name. INDEPENDENCE, when I follow your dictates blindly, I am giving self-will a frightening opportunity to grow out of hand. The more I remove myself from the gentle dictates of others, the more I listen to the clamorous cries to serve myself. In every YES to you there is greater bondage.

In community there are so many wills to alter my own, to shift my viewpoints, to keep me pliable and yielding. Community provides fertile soil for wholesale growth while bowing and bending to the many winds of diversity and adversity. In independent seclusion I can grow crooked and bent with no other plants in my secluded garden to compare growth. INDEPENDENCE, you make me think out everything for myself. You don't allow me to yield and follow the mode, to be supple and be led. I can never follow the wind, I must always walk against it. I can never sing the melody, but always the countermelody. Is all this opposition to the mainstream of living taking me anywhere? I don't know why I follow all the lone roads you lay before me, INDEPENDENCE. At the end of today's travel, there will not be an inn of fellowship awaiting. If I protest, you will have arguments ready to show me that I was destined to walk alone, that my personality demands it, that my chosen work demands it, and in my weariness of fighting you I will surrender and listen attentively to your next plan of the solitary way.

What can I do? I want to see a flicker of hope in my plight. If only for one time, I am going to become independent of you, INDEPENDENCE. I hear footsteps and a gentle voice that says, "Come, follow me." I am going.

Despondency

DESPONDENCY, you have a way of spreading a melancholy gray cast over the brightest of skies and turning my whole world sunless. You strike at that vital lifeline that holds me to the belief that God cares for me. When you manage to cut that line, I am truly destitute and afloat on the sea of hopelessness.

Nothing seems worthwhile from this point onward. There is no longer value in anything, not even in accepting God's will for the moment, for in your grip I am numb, and cannot feel the presence of the God you have obscured from me. Reason, strengthened by faith, is no match for your wiles.

I cannot understand how you get such a strong hold on me. Before I realize it, you have me defenseless. The more I fight, the less reason I see for the struggle. I want to be vibrant, alive, and eager for life, but I cannot pretend. I cannot ignite these qualities from another's enkindling.

I know that you will pass in time, as you always have, DESPONDENCY, but in the meanwhile I don't want my time to be wasted in this grayness. So I lift my sadness to a God I cannot feel, and ask that it may serve him in some way. If there is no perfume of prayer left in this earthen vessel, the lingering fragrance of what used to be will be enough for him to understand what I mean.

I will not grow anxious over my despondent state. I will use it as contrast to make me recall beauty I have once known. I will look at my leaden sky and thank God for all the azure skies he has blessed me with. I will look at my parched, thirsty grass and thank God for all the green pastures he has led me through. I will look at my heavy heart, and I will thank him for all the times my heart has known the rapture of his presence. DESPONDENCY, you have become the neutral canvas upon which I paint my gratefulness.

Talkativeness

TALKATIVENESS, you are an incessant instrument of my unrest. You endlessly seek receivers for your endless flow of words. Why don't you let my heart confide in the only One who can really understand, the only One in complete empathy with me? Why must you generate words from my mouth like a perpetual dynamo, words that inundate others without ever penetrating their interest?

When the dregs in the cup that he asks me to drink are too bitter, what is accomplished by repeated accounts of it to others? Why don't I just speak to him who gave me the cup? When the effervescent cup of joy is too much to hold without sharing, why don't I direct the overflow to the only heart big enough to contain it with pure acceptance? When life's problems are complex and a labyrinth of possible solutions lies before me, I can replace all my indecision with one word — *Jesus.* When I have been rejected, it doesn't take an infinite vocabulary of adjectives to share the burden with others. All it takes is one word — *Jesus.* What a rest for me, what a rest for those who are the canvases of my artistry of words, if I reduce my talkativeness to that all-resplendent word, *Jesus.*

Smallness

SMALLNESS, I have let you disintegrate my life in countless ways. You clutter my heart with multitudes of tiny arrows which bleed my vigor, enthusiasm, and endurance. You light upon me with such a graceful descent that I don't feel your treachery. Yet, when I have allowed enough tiny irritations to assemble, their united force is strong enough to destroy my composure.

One major misfortune does not have the same power to cripple me that many small mishaps do. The small bombardments shatter my oneness and I am so divided that I cannot gather myself for defense. Each stimulus seems insignificant on its own, but I should understand by now that it gathers close relatives to grow in power. A small envy will combine forces with a small greed. A small pride will combine forces with a small anger.

SMALLNESS, I can't pretend that you don't matter. Rather, I must recombine you with different partners. Small envy could be combined with small detachment; small pride with small humility. Then the powers will be neutralized, and not able to gather the momentum that shatters me piece by piece and peace by peace.

SMALLNESS, you can also attune me to the small things many people miss in life. You can make me aware of tiny meadowlark notes, of faint cricket cheeps, of little chipmunk tracks. You can awaken me to quiet things: sunrises, whispering leaves, starlight. You can train me to a fine sensitivity for color: the blue of the jay, the blue of the violet, the blue of the child's eye. You can tune me to sensitivity of taste: the sweetness of the honeycomb, the tartness of the choke-cherry, the mellowness of the pumpkin.

But, most of all, use your fine tuning to enhance my awareness of people's needs. May I understand the different sounds of hurting humanity, see the varying colors of suffering and the nuances of joy. Sad is sad in a thousand varying shades; happy is happy in a thousand different tones. Let me be aware of the small differences, for only then will I have the proper word or touch for those who need my understanding. SMALLNESS, tune me to perfect pitch.

Inordinate Ambition

INORDINATE AMBITION, you are not realistic in estimating what I can do. You convince me to engage in competition that can only lead to failure. Without the native endowments of others, I fall behind long before reaching the goal line. Then the self-incrimination begins.

AMBITION, why don't you try to recognize the boundary lines? God did not expect me to compete in every race. He said he gave special gifts to each of us, and together we complement one another and become a complete community of people. When I enter every race, I am often a cumbersome cog in a wheel of smooth operation, because I really don't qualify. I lower the performance rate because of my inability.

But maybe the worst injustice you inflict upon me, INORDINATE AMBITION, is that you pull me in so many directions that I don't know where my true qualifications lie. I am tilling so many fields that I don't know what crops I ought to concentrate on. A lifetime could never develop all the suggestions that you hand me, AMBITION. Why must you create such an insatiable appetite in me for accomplishment? No matter how weary I am, no matter how much I want to lift up the flag of surrender, you keep urging me onward.

And for what goals? To be first in fields where the harvest is temporal, where the glory is empty and short-lived; where the gratification is unsatisfying, where expectations never meet their height.

There is only one way I can continue living with you, INORDINATE AMBITION, and that is to have you bring to fruition in me Jesus' request: "You must be perfect as your heavenly Father is perfect." If you will gather all your forces together and work toward that goal, I will follow. Then, though you work me way beyond my strength, though you compel me to go on beyond my immediate desire, I will openly consent to your plans, for your objective is now my reason for living, "to be perfect as my heavenly Father is perfect." No more opposing forces to scatter me to the four winds. I know what I want.

Defensiveness

DEFENSIVENESS, like steel armor you cover me. You don't leave an unprotected area for the outside world to touch me. You carefully select my words to leave no spaces for answers which would cut through your protection. You steel my facial expressions so they leave no latitude for daring retorts. I stand still and challenging like a barricade against a world I do not love or trust. I am an island so impregnable that I need not ever fear transgressors.

DEFENSIVENESS, you keep me so unquestioningly safe that people no longer try to break through the defenses. They sense the aura of your mistrusting, ironclad safeguards so strongly that they shrivel from your aloofness and are left with the impression that I don't care about them.

I do, though. You have instilled in me such horror of being hurt that I am not willing to take chances anymore. I wrap myself in you, DEFENSIVENESS, layer after layer, until the chance element is completely eliminated.

But I am a Christian, and my Leader does not teach a doctrine of defensiveness. He himself was defenseless. Defenseless as a baby whom the cold night air could have taken from us; defenseless before Judas' wiles; before Pilate, before the crucifying mobs, defenseless in the cold stone tomb. Not only was his life defenseless, so was his doctrine. "When one strikes you on one cheek, turn the other one so it can be struck, too. When someone takes your cloak, offer him your coat, too."

"Love your enemies," he tells us. Don't build walls around yourself so you can't feel the hate of others. Face their hate, not with a clenched fist but with an open hand of love and forgiveness. DEFENSIVENESS, Jesus would say to untense your face, to let it be unprepared and unguarded and open to any assault that may be forthcoming. Loosen the flexed muscles ready for combat. Give whatever is asked of you, full measure, and running over. I am constant witness to all that happens. This is what he would say. If he is not my Protector, then I have none. If I am his follower, can I expect to sidestep all hurt? Can I expect to tiptoe through life in my defensive armor, unscathed? No, DEFENSIVENESS, I must choose to replace you with defenselessness.

Dishonesty

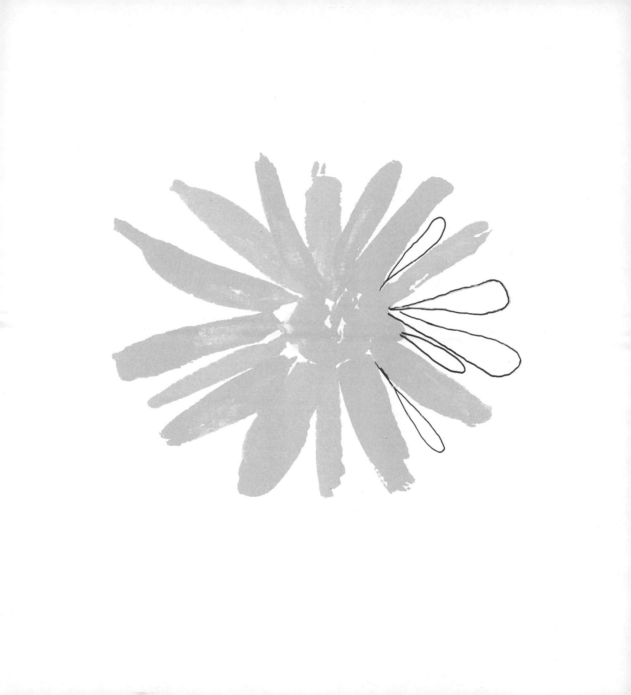

DISHONESTY, how I dread to admit that you are a part of me, but I detect your presence in small, disguised ways. I find traces of you in my conversation as I present truths slanted to my favor. You make me dishonest with myself in self-appraisals, excusing what I would never charitably overlook in others. You help me sidestep guilt in transgressions of commission and omission.

If I transgress God's law through uncharitable talk, you tell me it is my duty to enlighten others. If I transgress God's law by not defending justice, you congratulate me on my prudence.

I agree with someone on the surface because I am too lethargic and indifferent to present what I really feel on the subject, and let you assuage my torn conscience with your dishonest rationalizations. Deceitfulness, hypocrisy, feigned knowledge, feigned interest in others — all radiate from you, DISHONESTY. I believe I could detect traces of you in every vice I am trying to understand and handle efficiently. When I uproot you, I will have weakened the hold of all the vices. I ask Jesus to help me see truth unadorned, unmasked and uncomplicated.

Faithlessness

FAITHLESSNESS, what power could be mine if I could drive away your negativity. Faith, as small as the size of a mustard seed, is all I would need to move mountains! FAITHLESS-NESS, you are limiting my power tremendously. I will never move mountains or even people with your pernicious prompt-ings of "you can't, you can't, you can't."

You dim my hope for miracles, and I want to believe in them. When others are filled with expectant joy, I am lagging behind in the practical realm of what reason can prove. I want to dance through the unpredictable avenues of faith that defy logic, soar above understanding, and walk right over the practical.

But, as long as I listen to your weakening assertions, FAITHLESSNESS, I will never walk over the water. I will never know what it is like to have the salt spray from the sea of daringness whip my face while faith leads undaunted. You, with your conservative, well-measured permissions will keep me tied to your control. What did Jesus mean when he said, "Blessed are those who have not seen, yet believe"? Wasn't he striking at you, FAITHLESSNESS? You demand to have everything seen and proved before you believe.

I have tried to uproot you, but have failed. Must I, as the parable says, allow you to grow as a weed among my tender young plants of faith, lest in uprooting you I endanger the faith I am trying to nurture? Maybe you serve as an opposing force to make faith grow. I compare the soundings

66

of your conservatism to the adventurous daring of faith.
I compare your boundaries with the infinite horizons of faith,
and I can foresee that you will eventually be replaced by
faith. Lord, I want to move mountains in your name.

Excessiveness

EXCESSIVENESS, you diminish my visibility and cause me to career back and forth between extremes. When I witness moderation and practical planning you scoff at the grayness of such a dull existence.

You influence many areas. When I am angry how quickly you gather dry wood and throw it on the embryonic sparks and persuade them into a great conflagration. When I am envious of another's good fortune, how quickly you pour in to dilute my own unfortunate plight by contrast. When despair threatens you blanket me in a shroud of hopelessness and ruthlessly command me to suffer in unreasonable extremes.

When I am hungry, you lead me beyond what I need to be nourished. When I am lonely, you push me beyond what I need to feel one in the mainstream of humanity. When I am hurt you pull me beyond what I need to be healed. In this surfeiting my second state is often more hurtful than the first.

When I launch into a new undertaking, I call on prudence and temperance to fight you, EXCESSIVENESS, but often you gain momentum before I recognize you in your incipient stages. Then it is too late to stop your racing motor. Reason tells me how preposterous are your goals, but I am exhausted and empty, like a helpless puppet on a string. I bow and bend to many foolish, enervating expenditures of energies.

I stood adamantly against you, but you ran right over

the top of my refusals. Why must you obliterate my reason so that a middle position has no fascination for me?

You, EXCESSIVENESS, also force out of me one more song, one more word, one more appointment, one more act of forgiveness. You force me into deep waters while others stand close to the shores. You make me walk through dark valleys while others wait in the sunshine. You lead me down labyrinthian ways while others travel the main roads. I have much practice in suffering extremes because of you.

I thank you for this in one respect. The experience you have given me can be used to follow Jesus Christ through all the extremes of adversity, through turbulent waters of unknowing, through burning sands of aridity, through intricate paths of complex life plans. Pull me through all this, and drop me at the blessed feet of Excessive Love, the Lord my God.

Conflicting Selves

CONFLICTING SELVES, you make me a broken entity. I fall prey to so many vicissitudes of life because I am so divided within. Maybe the wanderlust of me needs the staying part of me to equalize forces, lest I gaze into ethereal visions and never live the practical moment at hand. Maybe the generous part of me needs the selfish part of me to keep me from flinging the doors of my heart too wantonly open, making it a marketplace of dissolution and waste. The defensive part of me needs the defenseless part of me lest I become a stone bulwark, undaunted and unconcerned about others.

Maybe the openness of me needs the closed self, lest I unreel my life before an audience that has no interest in viewing it.

The driving part of me needs the driver or there can be no movement forward. The willing needs the unwilling or there is no evaluating discretion preceding my actions. The shallow self needs the profound self or I find myself on a monotonous plateau.

I feel like a multitude of selves, each seeking to realize its essential nature. As in a courtroom, I listen to the various defenses, trying to discern the most justified plea.

I want to see a clear image emerge from the developer; I am weary of staying in the darkroom of my heart waiting for this image. Am I the driver or the driven; the leader or the led; the open or the closed? I want to see myself as an explicit entity. I want to recognize myself in a crowd. I want to be a unified fact. If only one side of my dual complements could win a decisive victory. . . .

Just when I think I am a leader, I see that I am following. When I decide that I really am a quiet, retiring person, I find words glibly tumbling from my mouth in unkempt profusion. In my confusion concerning which self is the real me, I begin to wonder if it should really matter. I think of a prayer I once read which said, "May they look at me and see Jesus Christ."

If that could be my constant prayer, Jesus would arrange all my conflicting selves into a balancing oneness that would eventually crystallize into an image that would be resplendent with his Light. O CONFLICTING SELVES, let us surrender to his unifying touch.

Passiveness

PASSIVENESS, how many shadows you have kept me in, telling me I must wait for an invitation to the light. I stand, outstretched heart hidden within me, begging to be invited to live. I feel I have something to offer life, but you convince me that I must wait to be discovered, that I must be drawn out by invitation only. Meanwhile my potential withers and diminishes.

PASSIVENESS, perhaps you are not only timid hesitation. Perhaps you are fear that your contribution to life is inadequate. Perhaps you are pride protecting yourself from hurtful exposure. Perhaps you are lethargy waiting for the flame of others' zeal to ignite your damp-wood heart into active participation in life.

Whatever form you take, you are causing me to lose many hours of service to God and to his people. I see the need to console, and you tell me that I should let God wipe away the tears, that it isn't time to stop crying yet. I see someone accused, and you tell me to wait for a sign to intervene. I see where a talent of mine could complete the mosaic of a noble work in progress, and you convince me that my contribution might not fit the scheme. So I relax into my pregnant nothingness.

I want to DO something. I not only want to be where the action is; I want to be the action. I don't want to wait to be lit by the torch of invitation; I want to be the torch that ignites truth, knowledge, courage, wisdom, and love. I want

78

to set the world on fire with love for Jesus who gave these invitations: Come, follow me. Come, I will make you fishers of men. Come, I will give you rest. Come, drink of Living Water.

My passive soul, why do you tarry under the cringing hesitation of PASSIVENESS? You have been invited, you have been invited by Life himself.

Fear of Suffering

FEAR OF SUFFERING, you are always protectively around me like a hand cupping a flame from treacherous winds. You suggest refuges from pain, discomfort, embarrassment or misunderstanding. Yet, there is a part of me that sees value in facing suffering. Tears in my eyes give me a clearer focus of life; tears spilling over my soul make it a reflector of the Father.

If my own actions have brought suffering upon me, I want to remain in this crucible of my own making until I am refined and closer to what I know I ought to be. If circumstances beyond me have brought the suffering, I want to remain in the crucible of his making until he feels I am what I ought to be.

FEAR OF SUFFERING, you constantly whisper solutions, all kinds of empty escapes: parties, distracting music, friends and more friends, drink, drugs, hyperactivity—anything to crowd the moments, to numb the spirit within me. You would keep me running breathlessly down one blind way after another, running without looking, just so suffering cannot catch up with me.

This alarming chase is worse than being caught. Most of what I am running from will never materialize. Your warnings have proven to be whims of negative imagination too often. I know, too, that the more I accept suffering, the more I feel the unison of heartbeats with the Son of God who was not spared suffering. The lashes of suffering hurt more at a distance than they do nearer the source of the lash. Distance adds momentum to the swing.

I will not purposely walk into a field of suffering, but no longer am I going to run from it. If to follow Jesus I must walk through the valley of darkness, I am not going to waste hours trying to find a sunny detour. If I feel that suffering is pursuing me, I am not going to run, but instead I will let it engulf me, for with it will come the grace I need to endure it. I believe his words: "My grace is sufficient for you." I will emerge from the encounter better equipped to conquer the next.

FEAR OF SUFFERING, how many agonizing moments of anxiety you have unnecessarily laid on my enslaved heart. How many sunrises I could not welcome because you held me sleepless in your inexorable grip all night. How many resplendent sunsets I never even noticed because you had my sight colored with the dye of fright. How many voices called to me that I never heard because the tirade of your fright-evoking words eclipsed all other sound. How often you made me stand shivering on the shores of life while others fearlessly and joyously dipped into the sea of life.

If I really believe that God tempers the wind to the shorn lamb, I won't fastidiously measure the velocity of the headwinds; if I really believe his words: "BEHOLD, I AM WITH YOU ALWAYS" I won't fear loneliness. If I really believe his words: "COME TO ME, I WILL GIVE YOU REST,"

I won't fear having no one to turn to. If I really believe his words: "PEACE, I GIVE, BUT NOT AS THE WORLD GIVES," I will believe that there is for me an inward stillness that all the sounds of a wildly pulsating world cannot shatter.

If he ordains that I must suffer, I know I can find that peace even in the crucible of suffering. Scripture reassures me that all the sufferings in the whole world are not worthy to be compared to the joy that God has prepared for those who are faithful.

O SUFFERING, where is your sting? O FEAR OF SUFFERING, where is your power?

To the Son

Jesus, you know what it is to be human. Born as one of us, you know what each of us suffers in our humanity. I have in my heart the blueprint of what I want to be, and I think it matches the one the Father holds in his hand. I believe he gives me sufficient glimpses to know. I desire to fit this image perfectly, but I see at last that I cannot do this without your ever-present help. Left to myself I cannot control the opposing forces that blur my vision. I have spoken to these disintegrating forces that threaten to tear me apart, and it seems I have put them into order and submission. But I know their power to rise into control again. In an unguarded moment I can be once again enslaved to their dictates.

Through the enlightenment of the Spirit of God I am brought to this triumphant revelation: Without you I can do nothing; with you I can do all things. You tell me that your grace is sufficient. It is sufficient for me to bring myself to the completion of the Father's plan for me so that, when at last God holds me in his right hand, the blueprint in his left will be perfectly met. My hunger for wholeness in him will then be forever satisfied.